Nehe
BUILDER FOR GOD

The Story of Nehemiah
accurately retold from the Bible
(from the Book of Nehemiah), by
NEIL M. ROSS

Design and Illustrations
Duncan McLaren
Mackay Design Associates Ltd

Published in Great Britain by
CHRISTIAN FOCUS PUBLICATIONS LTD
Geanies House, Fearn, Tain, Ross-shire IV20 1TW, Scotland
http://www.christianfocus.com
© 1983 Christian Focus Publications Ltd ISBN 0 906731 11 9

New edition 1988.

Reprinted 1992

Reprinted 1998

Long ago, in the land of Persia, there was a rich and noble Jew called Nehemiah who loved and worshipped God.

He was the important servant,
called The Cup-bearer, of King
Artaxerxes of Persia and served
the king's wine to him.

King Artaxerxes ruled over many lands. One of these lands was Judah where the Jews lived and where the famous city of Jerusalem was.

One day, some Jews from Judah visited Nehemiah and gave him sad news.

They told him that the Jews there were being cruelly treated by their enemies and that the wall and city gates of Jerusalem were in ruins.

Nehemiah wept after hearing this. What could he do? He did the best thing he could have done, for he prayed to God about it. He asked God to help him to do something for the Jews.

One day after this, Nehemiah was
very sad as he served wine to
King Artaxerxes.

"Why do you look sad?" the king
suddenly asked him.

Nehemiah told the king the bad
news about the ruined wall and
gates of Jerusalem.

"What do you want?" asked the king.

Right away, Nehemiah prayed silently to God for help and then asked the king, "Please send me to Jerusalem to build its wall".

What do you think happened? The king not only granted him his wish but even made him Governor of Judah. How wonderfully God answered Nehemiah's prayers.

Do you have difficulties and troubles? Take them to the Lord in prayer because He can answer your prayers too.

When Nehemiah came to Jerusalem, two men were very displeased that he had come to help the Jews. Their names were Sanballat and Tobiah and they hated the Jews.

One night, soon after he came to
Jerusalem, Nehemiah and some of
his men secretly went to see how
much work would have to be done
to mend the city wall. How badly
broken down it was! Heaps of
stones and other rubble lay all
around.

Nehemiah went to the chief men of the city and said, "Come and let us build up the wall of Jerusalem!" When they heard from Nehemiah how God had been helping him they were glad and wanted to start building.

So Nehemiah and the people began to build the wall. What a difficult job they had to do! The heaps of rubble had to be cleared away. The wall had to be built very high and wide right round the city. The Sheep Gate, the East Gate and the other eight gates of the city all had to be repaired.

Sanballat was in a rage at the Jews when he saw them start to build and he said that the wall would be useless. Tobiah also mocked them and said, "Even a fox, if it went up on the wall, would break it down".

But Nehemiah trusted in God and prayed to Him again for help. God answered Nehemiah's prayer and helped them to work so well that soon half of the huge wall was finished.

Sanballat and his wicked friends now became very angry. They made a plan to suddenly attack the Jews and stop them building.

Nehemiah heard about their wicked plan and prayed to God about that too. Then he made a plan to defend the city.

He ordered half the men to take their weapons and guard the city. The others were to keep on working but with their swords beside them. They were all to defend the city as soon as the trumpet would sound at the command of Nehemiah.

Because Nehemiah was trusting in God to help them in battle he told the people, "Our God shall fight for us". So the work went on and at the same time the city was guarded day and night. The men did not take off their clothes even at night, except to wash, so that they were always ready to fight.

Nehemiah had another worry at this time. Some rich Jews lent money to many of the Jews who were poor. But they also took the land, houses and even the children from these poor Jews until the money was paid back. This was very wrong because God commanded them not to treat their brother Jews in this way.

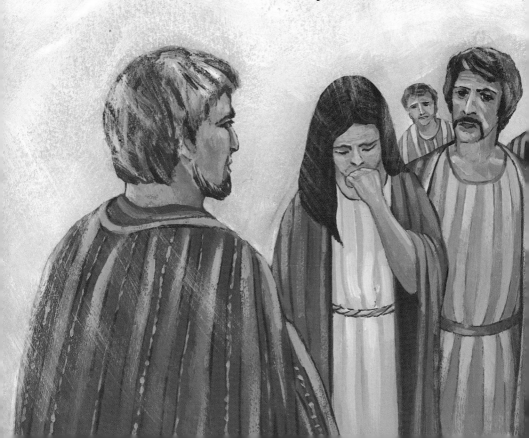

The poor Jews told Nehemiah about it and asked him to help them. Nehemiah told the rich Jews, "What you are doing is not good!" and pleaded with them to have pity on the poor Jews.

When the poor Jews heard that the rich Jews promised to give back their property and children they were very glad and praised God.

We also must pity the poor. God says to everyone that those who pity the poor lend to Him and that He will pay them back.

The wall was now nearly finished and Sanballat and Tobiah suddenly became very friendly to Nehemiah. They actually invited him to come down to visit them. Were they really friendly? Not at all, for they were secretly plotting to hurt him.

Nehemiah refused their invitation and sent a message to them saying, "I am doing a great work, so that I cannot come down".

Sanballat tried other evil tricks to frighten Nehemiah and stop the work, but each time Nehemiah asked God for help. So the people were helped to work on and on until the wall was finished.

Do you know how long they took to build that great wall? Only 52 days, because God made them willing and strong to build the wall of His city.

Some time after that, all the people, children as well, met together in one of the streets of the city to worship God. Ezra the priest and some of the other priests stood on a big wooden pulpit in front of the people and read and explained God's law to them.

We too must meet together to hear God's word, the Bible, explained to us by God's messengers, the preachers of the gospel.

When the people understood the meaning of God's word they worshipped God in the way that He wanted. They kept the holy feasts and they were really sorry to God for their sins.

We also must be truly sorry to God for our sins and ask Him to forgive us for Jesus' sake.

After that, the people promised
God that they would keep his
laws. This promise was written
down and Nehemiah and other
chief men wrote their names under it.

There was another big gathering
of the people: this time to thank
God for helping them to build the wall.

What a happy day that was!
Thousands of men, women and
children, led by Nehemiah and the
princes and the priests, praised
God with such great joy that they
were heard by those who lived far
away from the city.

We too should be thanking God for His goodness and especially for His greatest gift. What is that gift? It is the gift of His dear Son, Jesus Christ, whom He gave to save sinners.

After that happy day Nehemiah carried on governing Judah for some years and then went back to Persia.

But Nehemiah did come back to visit Jerusalem some time later. During that visit he saw some things which made him sad.

He saw that one of the rooms in God's holy temple had been given to wicked Tobiah to live in. Nehemiah was very upset. He threw Tobiah's belongings out of the temple and did not allow him to live there any longer.

Nehemiah also saw many of the people doing work on the Sabbath day that God had forbidden them to do on that holy day. He told the people how wrong they were. He also ordered the merchants, who came to the city to sell their goods on the Sabbath day, to go away. They did not come back again on God's day to sell.

We too must not do what God forbids us to do on His holy day, the Lord's Day, which is the Sabbath day of Christians. God still commands us, "Remember the sabbath day, to keep it holy"

There was another thing which made Nehemiah sad. Many Jews had married heathen people.

God had forbidden them to do this because the heathen did not worship Him but worshipped idols.

Nehemiah punished those Jews and made the people promise that they would not allow their sons or daughters to marry heathen people.

Once more, Nehemiah put right
some things that were wrong,
praying to God for help to do so.

We see then that Nehemiah was a
man who worked very hard for
God and for God's people.

He was also a very brave man for
he kept doing what was right even
when some people hated him for
that.

We must follow his example and
do what God tells us to do, even
when others try to stop us.

Above all, Nehemiah was a man of prayer. Again and again he asked God for His help and blessing and God answered his prayers.

Nehemiah wrote a book called *The Book of Nehemiah*, which you will find in the Bible. There you can read the story of Nehemiah and his work.

The last words of *The Book of Nehemiah* are a prayer that Nehemiah prayed.

You too can pray that prayer, for God promises you, "Ask and you shall receive".

Here is the prayer, "Remember me, O my God, for good".